Bay of Islands
A PARADISE FOUND

Photography: Frank Habicht

Narration: Bob Molloy

TOTARA PRESS

Frank Habicht

Internationally known photographer Frank Habicht many years ago fell in love with the Bay of Islands and has since never stopped putting his love affair on film. Born in Hamburg, Frank worked in London and Berlin and has been published extensively in New Zealand and Europe.

Bob Molloy

UK-born Bob Molloy, an award-winning journalist who later turned to publishing, has a fellow feeling for Northland and the Bay of Islands in particular. Having spent most life in the writing game he moved to newspaper publishing. Like Frank he too discovered the Bay of Islands and has lived here ever since.

First published in New Zealand by Totara Press
6 School Road, Paihia, Bay of Islands, New Zealand.
Facsimile: 0-9-402 8238

Photographer: Frank Habicht
Narrator: Bob Molloy
Book Cover and Design: Garry Whitham
Imaging and Printing: Calders Design & Print Co., Whangarei.

ISBN 0-908817-21-5

Bay of Islands
A PARADISE FOUND

A Brief History of the Bay of Islands

Tucked away in the north-east corner of the North Island *of* New Zealand *is a sub-tropical paradise where dozens of islands cradle in the sun.* Named *the* Bay *of* Islands *by* Captain Cook *on his first voyage of discovery in the late 18th century, it is today a quiet paradise where visitors enjoy its pristine islands and scenic beauty.*

But it wasn't always like that. When Cook *arrived he found it well populated with* Maori *families who lived in fortified villages on hilltops around the coastline and on each of the the main islands.* They *fished the oceans, harvested shellfish, and cultivated large vegetable gardens in a life of constant vigilance that befitted a warrior culture.*

The *militant aspect of their lives was governed by the concept of utu, revenge for real or imaged wrongs.* Early Maori *were non-literate people.* Reading *and writing were unknown.* History *and learning was oral, passed on from generation to generation in songs, stories and lists of genealogies.* Utu *was maintained by remembrance of wrongs, also passed on orally from one generation to another, leading on occasion to inter-tribal and even inter-family wars and clashes.*

It *was this proud warrior culture that greeted* Cook *on his arrival.* His *visit got off to a shaky start when several of his sailors plundered an island garden for much needed vegetables and were attacked by the owners.* Talks *with local chiefs smoothed the misunderstanding and the remainder of his visit was peaceful.* Joseph Banks, *the botanist who sailed with* Cook *on this voyage, noted in his journal that the bay was "more thickly populated than those parts further south, the people more elaborately tattooed, the canoes more elaborately carved, the bay itself beautiful with many good anchorages, the hills and valleys round it, the forests and cultivations beautiful also."*

After Cook's *visit the southern oceans became a happy hunting ground for whalers and traders who increasingly called in at the* Bay *to take on fresh water and food.* With *them came liquor and muskets.* Guns *were much prized by militant* Maori *who saw in them a means of overcoming their enemies.* This *trade rapidly upset the tribal balance.* Soon *war parties armed with muskets were raiding the land far to the south, killing and enslaving their tribal cousins.*

Liquor too had its inevitable effect. A *rough and ready settlement of grog shops and brothels sprang up on the site of the present day* Russell, *little more than a hide-out for escaped convicts from* Australia, *mutinous sailors and drifters.* Dubbed *the* "Hell Hole *of the* Pacific" *by the whaler captains, who had difficulty disciplining their crews there after months at sea, it was described by one visitor as "notorious at present for containing a greater number of rogues than any other spot of equal size in the universe".*

On the heels of the whalers came the missionaries, opening tiny mission stations on the opposite shores of the bay, bringing artisan skills and the Bible to their converts. An uneasy relationship separated the rapidly growing trader communities and the missionaries who soon saw the need for some form of rule of law to protect Maori.

This came in 1840 with the Treaty of Waitangi in which some 50 chiefs signed over sovereignty of their land to Britain in return for equal citizenship for all under British law. The treaty was subsequently extended by chiefs throughout the country to cover the whole of New Zealand.

Following some hiccups and false starts, during which Russell - then known as Kororareka - was sacked and burned by Maori warriors, the bay settled into more peaceful times. A rush of get-rich-quick tree felling in the late 1800s destroyed most of the surrounding forest, followed by gum diggers who fossicked the cleared land for fossil kauri gum. Farming grassed over the open landscapes, creating the tree-lined paddocks which are a feature of the bay today. Farming and fishing remained the main occupations until early in the 20th century when horticulture took advantage of the rich volcanic soils around Kerikeri.

Today the village of Russell drowses in the sun, its rowdy history written on the gravestones in the little church yard and on the church walls by musket balls. The bay population is concentrated mainly in the surrounding townships of Kawakawa, Paihia, Kerikeri and Waipapa.

A major industry is tourism. Visitors have a choice of uncrowded sandy beaches, dreamy islands, a range of fishing from the largest of the big game to river and lake trout, and a wealth of shellfish, crayfish, oysters and scallops. Boating is a major recreation and most residents have access to the water in some form or another.

An idyllic place indeed, a friendly spot where people stop to talk, where open spaces and pristine water are just part of the scenery, and the air is always clean and fresh.

Welcome then to the Bay of Idylls…

Where the Tasman Sea and the Pacific Ocean meet, lies a place of enhanced natural beauty – the Bay of Islands. For me, it is Earth's last unspoiled paradise.

We celebrate life with its diversity of people and scenery. Nature is soothing, tranquillity abounds, here we embrace the dawn, touch the moon and the stars are within reach. Sun lights green hills, clouds drift across deep and blue seas – in a world so old.

We breathe pure air 24 hours a day, swim with the dolphins, follow the trail of the mighty striped marlin through rainbows of spray, to the endless ocean. Our people live in harmony and tolerance – a true Family of Man.

Old traditions are valued. Maori mythology tells of love, sea, sky and land. Elders are respected for their wisdom and insight, children are loved for their charm and innocence.

A new millennium dawns. We jump with joy into the new day. Can we ask for more?

Haere Mai – Welcome here.

Frank Habicht

As the first dawn lit Aotearoa
- paradise was discovered

Maori were masters of the sea

Then others came to share paradise

TRADEWIND

A canoe journey requires thought

As do journeys of the mind

Ceremony is powerful

And loud

While fun and laughter

Holds us posed for more

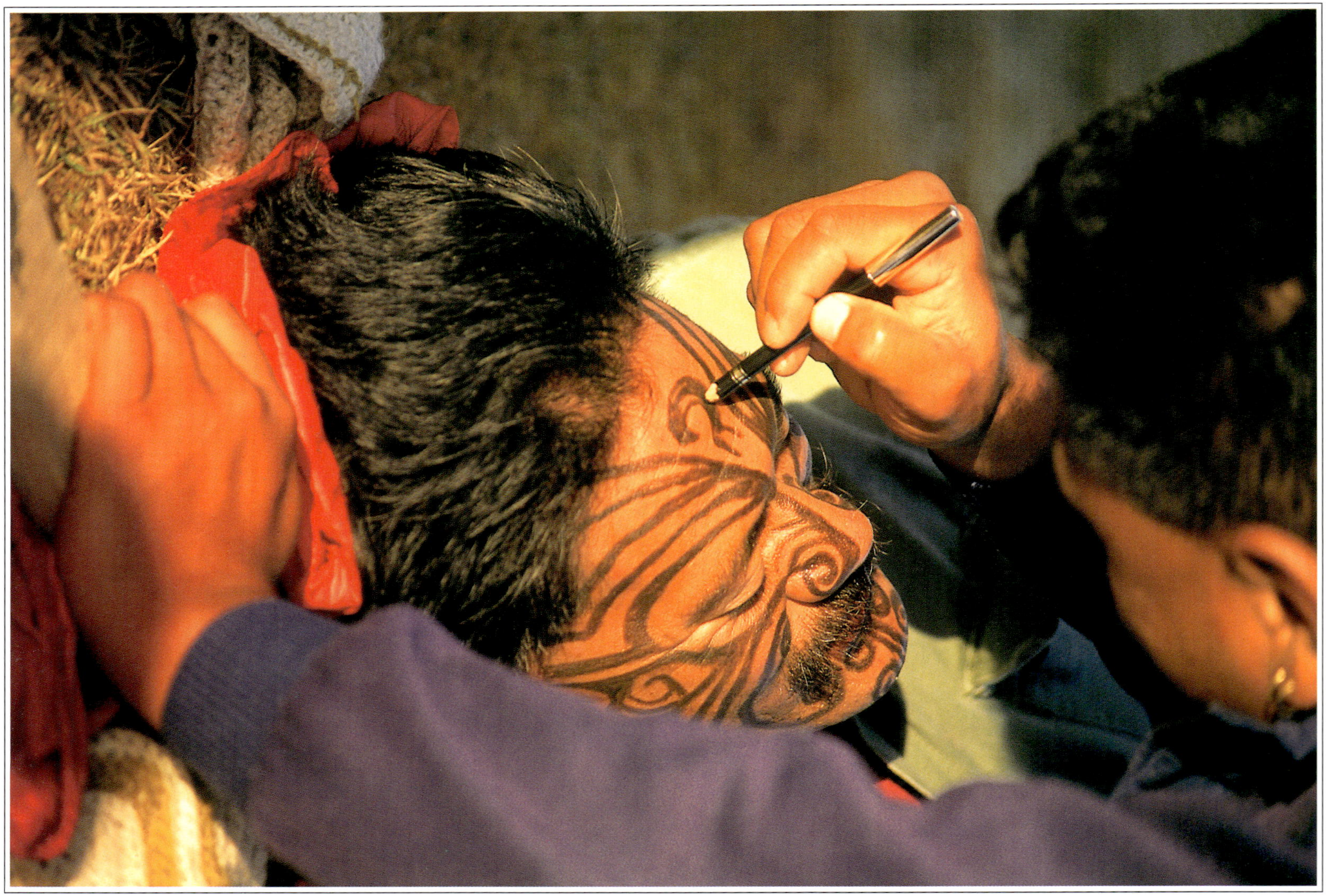

Getting ready takes time

But *results are worthwhile*

Because we like

To look our best

We can make

Our visitors smile

We like to fly the right flag

And pace out the borders

Regardless…

The celebration goes on

Now and then the mood changes

Mostly we have fun

But, for some, long thoughts…

TUCKER THOMPSON

Different ways…

To see the country

And historic places

Where cultures meet

Gardens smile

And clerics too

Even the famous

And their friends

Serene seascapes invite

Beach walks delight

Houses are colourful

And homes are open

Landscapes to die for

And to live for

Horses wear the right gear

A bit less if you're a calf

Paradise is so beautiful

That we just let it wash over us

And where God smiles

Trees grow

We walk…

On the bright side

Everyday routine…

Has its beauty

Paradise has many delights

And sights

A churchyard for rest

And a river to fish

Memories rest well

In quiet landscapes

While under a peaceful flag

A *great artist*

Children dress for play

And fun

We've got them old…

Railway blues

Marriages may be made in heaven

But we have weddings in paradise

The food is good, the wine superb

And the service just incredible

Fruit ripens

Flowers bloom

A tree in the meadow

And another wedding in paradise

Make for frolics in the sun

And memories on the grass

Girls run

And climb

Boys challenge

Girls smile

Beauty unending

Landscapes drenched in colour

Evening falls

But Paradise never closes down

Index